How to Properly Talk to God

By Dr. Ruth M. Wilson

BK Royston Publishing LLC
Jeffersonville, IN

BK Royston Publishing
P. O. Box 4321
Jeffersonville, IN 47131
502-802-5385
http://bkroystonpublishing.com

Cover DESIGNER: TED DONES
TLD GRAPHIC DESIGN
417.396.8295 | P.O.BOX 43881
LOUISVILLE, KY 40243
WWW.MESSENGERSOFFIRE.ORG

ISBN-13: 978-0692728260
ISBN-10: 0692728260

All Scriptures are taken from the KING JAMES
VERSION (KJV): public domain or from the
version of the bible listed and within the
permission for use guidelines.

Printed in the United States of America

Dedication

This book is dedicated to Shekinah Glory Ministries for making it possible for me to take this time to get away and write. I love you guys!

To every person who wants to talk to God but doesn't know how, may this be a blessing to you.

Last but surely not least to every person that has ever prayed for me, thank you from the bottom of my heart. For the prayers of the righteous availeth much!

Call unto me and I will answer thee, and shew thee great and mighty things, which thou knowest not. Jeremiah 33:3

Table of Contents

Introduction

This book is designed to teach God's children how to pray properly and effectively. Even the Word of God says, "We don't know how to pray as we ought."

Romans 8:26
Likewise the Spirit also helpeth our infirmities: for we know not what we should pray for as we ought: but the Spirit itself maketh intercession for us with groanings which cannot be uttered.

Turn the pages and let's learn how to *Properly Talk to God*.

What Is Prayer
Chapter 1

It is a personal conversation not
just to God, but with God, yes a
dialogue. When you talk to Him, He
will talk back to you. You just have
to be able to recognize His voice.
That's another book, "The Voice of
God", but God speaks orally, when
you can hear him as you would
hear any human's voice. He
speaks within you, "Your
spirit/heart", through his Word,
through his leaders (pastors,
teachers, evangelists, prophets
and apostles), through others and
even children.

Prayer is acknowledgement, adoration, thanksgiving, confession, intercession, supplication, and conclusion.

Acknowledge is to regard or describe (someone or something) as having or deserving a particular status

Adoration is a deep love and respect for who God is

Thanksgiving is an expression of gratitude to God.

Confession is an admission or acknowledgement that I am guilty of doing something that goes against God's laws/ways.

Intercession is the action of intervening on behalf of another.

Supplication is the action of asking for something earnestly or humbly.

Conclusion ending the prayer

In Luke 11 one of the disciples asked the Lord to teach them how to pray as John had taught his disciples and Jesus response was.

Luke 11:1-4
And it came to pass, that, as he was praying in a certain place, when he ceased, one of his disciples said unto him, Lord, teach us to pray, as John also taught his disciples.

[2] And he said unto them, When ye pray, say, Our Father which art in heaven,(Acknowledgement of who he is) Hallowed be thy name.(Reference) Thy kingdom come. Thy will be done, as in heaven, so in earth. (Submission to His will)

[3] Give us day by day our daily bread. (Divine supply spiritual and natural)

[4] And forgive us our sins; (Repentance) for we also forgive every one that is indebted to us. (Forgiveness)

[5]And lead us not into temptation; (Divine restraint) but deliver us from evil. (Deliverance sought)

Acknowledge/ Address is how we start the prayer off
Father - Father God – God - Lord
Jehovah - Elohim
Creator

Or whatever your favorite name for God is.

Isaiah 45:5
I am the LORD, and there is none else, there is no God beside me: I girded thee, though thou hast not known me:

Psalm 83:18
That men may know that thou, whose name alone is JEHOVAH, art the most high over all the earth.

Revelation 1:8
I am Alpha and Omega, the beginning and the ending, saith the Lord, which is, and which was, and which is to come, the Almighty.

Exodus 34:14
For thou shalt worship no other god: for the LORD, whose name is Jealous, is a jealous God:

Adoration, deep love and respect for who God is

1 Chronicles 29:11-14
Thine, O LORD is the greatness, and the power, and the glory, and the victory, and the majesty: for all that is in the heaven and in the earth is thine; thine is the kingdom, O LORD, and thou art exalted as head above all.

[12] Both riches and honour come of thee, and thou reignest over all; and in thine hand is power and might; and in thine hand it is to make great, and to give strength unto all.

[13] Now therefore, our God, we thank thee, and praise thy glorious name.

Revelation 5:13
And every creature which is in heaven, and on the earth, and under the earth, and such as are in the sea, and all that are in them, heard I saying, Blessing, and honour, and glory, and power, be unto him that sitteth upon the throne, and unto the Lamb for ever and ever.

Just tell Him who and what He is to you.

Thanksgiving is an expression of gratitude to God.

Ephesians 5:20
Giving thanks always for all things unto God and the Father in the name of our Lord Jesus Christ;

I Thessalonians 5:18
In everything give thanks: for this is the will of God in Christ Jesus concerning you.
It doesn't matter what happens in your life, be thankful anyway and watch God work it out for your good. This is His will and way of doing things, wanting us to trust him, because we belong to him now.

Psalm 107:1
O give thanks unto the LORD, for he is good: for his mercy endureth forever.

Psalm 100:4
Enter into his gates with thanksgiving, and into his courts with praise: be thankful unto him, and bless his name.

Thank him for everything you can think of from a new day, his provision, his grace, his mercy, his love, whatever you are thankful for.

Confession is an admission or acknowledgement that I am guilty of doing something that goes against God's laws/ways.

1 John 1:9
If we confess our sins, he is faithful and just to forgive us our sins, and to cleanse us from all unrighteousness.

James 5:16
Confess your faults one to another, and pray one for another, that ye may be healed. The effectual fervent prayer of a righteous man availeth much.

Proverbs 28:13
He that covereth his sins shall not prosper: but whoso confesseth and forsaketh them shall have mercy.

Anyone who refuses to admit his mistakes will never become who you were created to be nor will you be successful. If you confess and turn away from your sins/mistakes, you will find that God is a God of another chance.

Intercession is the action of intervening on behalf of another.

1 Timothy 2:1
I exhort therefore, that, first of all, supplications, prayers, intercessions, and giving of thanks, be made for all men;

These are God's instructions and directions: Pray unselfishly, pray for others; from our spiritual leaders, to our world leaders, government, teachers, family, sinners, thanking him for all he is doing in and for them.

Numbers 21:7
Therefore the people came to Moses, and said, We have sinned, for we have spoken against the LORD, and against thee; pray unto the LORD, that he take away the serpents from us. And Moses prayed for the people.

Matthew 5:44
But I say unto you, Love your enemies, bless them that curse you, do good to them that hate you, and pray for them which despitefully use you, and persecute you;

Supplication is the action of asking for something earnestly or humbly.

Hebrews 4:16
Let us therefore come boldly unto the throne of grace, that we may obtain mercy, and find grace to help in time of need.

Philippians 4:19
But my God shall supply all your need according to his riches in glory by Christ Jesus.

Psalm 20:4-5
Grant thee according to thine own heart, and fulfil all thy counsel.

[5] We will rejoice in thy salvation, and in the name of our God we will set up our banners: the LORD fulfil all thy petitions.

Psalm 20:4-5
[4] May he grant you your heart's desire and fulfill all your plans. [5] May there be shouts of joy when we hear the news of your victory, flags flying with praise to God for all that he has done for you. May he answer all your prayers!

Mark 11:24

24 Therefore I say unto you, What things soever ye desire, when ye pray, believe that ye receive them, and ye shall have them.

Be specific when asking for what you need according to his will, remembering that He knows what you stand in need of before you ask. Also, those things that He has promised, just get in agreement with Him and thank Him that you have them.

Make sure to always end or
conclude the prayer
In Jesus name I pray, amen!

John 14:6
Jesus saith unto him, I am the way, the truth,
and the life: no man cometh unto the Father,
but by me.

Ephesians 2:18
For through him we both have access by one
Spirit unto the Father.

Why Should I Pray
Chapter 2

There are many reasons why we should PRAY/ talk to God.

One, it is our connection to Him.

Jeremiah 29:12-13 Then shall ye call upon me, and ye shall go and pray unto me, and I will hearken unto you. And ye shall seek me, and find me, when ye shall search for me with all your heart.

The Father says, when we pray, we'll have his undivided attention, but our hearts must be right. The more we talk with him the deeper our relationship will be. The more we talk with him we'll discover who, what and why we are. Last but not least, the more we talk to God, the enemy will be revealed/uncovered therefore, we will not be ignorant of his devices.

Secondly we need to know our **Creator**

Genesis 1:1; 27
In the beginning God created the heaven and the earth.
So God created man in his own image, in the image of God created he him; male and female created he them

He reveals himself to us, in his love, wisdom, and power when we pray.

Third, it is one of the ways we are transformed (changed/matured) strengtheneth.

Jude1: 20
But ye, beloved, building up yourselves on your most holy faith, praying in the Holy Ghost.
Through prayer the Father also shows us ourselves, weaknesses, strengths.

Fourth it will keep us out of trouble

Matthew 26:41
Watch and pray, that ye enter not into temptation: the spirit indeed is willing, but the flesh is weak.

Staying in prayer will keep us focused so that we won't get into trouble, (do the things we used to do.) The God in us wants to do the right thing, but the old nature wants to keep rising up.

Fifth it is how we get things done

Philippians 4:6

Be careful for nothing; but in every thing by prayer and supplication with thanksgiving let your requests be made known unto God.

Mark 11:24
Therefore I say unto you, What things soever ye desire, when ye pray, believe that ye receive them, and ye shall have them.

Matthew 7:7
Ask, and it shall be given you; seek, and ye shall find; knock, and it shall be opened unto you:

When we spend time alone with God, we can share anything with him. We can tell him about our concerns, our fears, our needs or what we desire, but don't forget to thank him for what he has already done and for what he will do.

Six prayer will cause us to rest and be at peace

Matthew 11:28
Come unto me, all ye that labour and are heavy laden, and I will give you rest.

Seven it helps us to operate in power and authority over the enemy.

Matthew 18:18-20
Verily I say unto you, Whatsoever ye shall bind on earth shall be bound in heaven: and whatsoever ye shall loose on earth shall be loosed in heaven. [19] Again I say unto you, That if two of you shall agree on earth as touching any thing that they shall ask, it shall be done for them of my Father which is in heaven. [20] For where two or three are gathered together in my name, there am I in the midst of them.

When two of us get together, whether it be you and another person or you and the Holy Ghost, and we agree about an issue/concern and pray about it, that's double faith and power. The Father immediately goes into

action on our behalf and he alone
gets the credit.

1 Samuel 17:32-54
*32 And David said to Saul, Let no man's heart
fail because of him; thy servant will go and fight
with this Philistine.*

*33 And Saul said to David, Thou art not able to
go against this Philistine to fight with him: for
thou art but a youth, and he a man of war from
his youth.*

*34 And David said unto Saul, Thy servant kept
his father's sheep, and there came a lion, and
a bear, and took a lamb out of the flock:*

*35 And I went out after him, and smote him, and
delivered it out of his mouth: and when he
arose against me, I caught him by his beard,
and smote him, and slew him.*

*36 Thy servant slew both the lion and the bear:
and this uncircumcised Philistine shall be as
one of them, seeing he hath defied the armies
of the living God.*

*37 David said moreover, The LORD that
delivered me out of the paw of the lion, and out
of the paw of the bear, he will deliver me out of*

the hand of this Philistine. And Saul said unto David, Go, and the LORD be with thee.

38 And Saul armed David with his armour, and he put an helmet of brass upon his head; also he armed him with a coat of mail.
39 And David girded his sword upon his armour, and he assayed to go; for he had not proved it. And David said unto Saul, I cannot go with these; for I have not proved them. And David put them off him.

40 And he took his staff in his hand, and chose him five smooth stones out of the brook, and put them in a shepherd's bag which he had, even in a scrip; and his sling was in his hand: and he drew near to the Philistine.

41 And the Philistine came on and drew near unto David; and the man that bare the shield went before him.

42 And when the Philistine looked about, and saw David, he disdained him: for he was but a youth, and ruddy, and of a fair countenance.

43 And the Philistine said unto David, Am I a dog, that thou comest to me with staves? And the Philistine cursed David by his gods.

44 And the Philistine said to David, Come to me, and I will give thy flesh unto the fowls of the air, and to the beasts of the field.

*45 Then said David to the Philistine, Thou comest to me with a sword, and with a spear, and with a shield: but I come to thee in the name of the LORD of hosts, the God of the armies of Israel, whom thou hast defied.
46 This day will the LORD deliver thee into mine hand; and I will smite thee, and take thine head from thee; and I will give the carcases of the host of the Philistines this day unto the fowls of the air, and to the wild beasts of the earth; that all the earth may know that there is a God in Israel.*

47 And all this assembly shall know that the LORD saveth not with sword and spear: for the battle is the LORD's, and he will give you into our hands.

48 And it came to pass, when the Philistine arose, and came, and drew nigh to meet David, that David hastened, and ran toward the army to meet the Philistine.

49 And David put his hand in his bag, and took thence a stone, and slang it, and smote the Philistine in his forehead, that the stone sunk into his forehead; and he fell upon his face to the earth.

50 So David prevailed over the Philistine with a sling and with a stone, and smote the Philistine, and slew him; but there was no sword in the hand of David.

51 Therefore David ran, and stood upon the Philistine, and took his sword, and drew it out of the sheath thereof, and slew him, and cut off his head therewith. And when the Philistines saw their champion was dead, they fled. 52 And the men of Israel and of Judah arose, and shouted, and pursued the Philistines, until thou come to the valley, and to the gates of Ekron. And the wounded of the Philistines fell down by the way to Shaaraim, even unto Gath, and unto Ekron.

53 And the children of Israel returned from chasing after the Philistines, and they spoiled their tents.

54 And David took the head of the Philistine, and brought it to Jerusalem; but he put his armour in his tent.

Eight it changes situations, opens doors, & causes healing in the land

Jeremiah 33:3
Call unto me and I will answer thee, and shew thee great and mighty things, which thou knowest not.

Acts 12:5-16

5 Peter therefore was kept in prison: but prayer was made without ceasing of the church unto God for him.

6 And when Herod would have brought him forth, the same night Peter was sleeping between two soldiers, bound with two chains: and the keepers before the door kept the prison.

7 And, behold, the angel of the Lord came upon him, and a light shined in the prison: and he smote Peter on the side, and raised him up, saying, Arise up quickly. And his chains fell off from his hands.

8 And the angel said unto him, Gird thyself, and bind on thy sandals. And so he did. And he saith unto him, Cast thy garment about thee, and follow me.

9 And he went out, and followed him; and wist not that it was true which was done by the angel; but thought he saw a vision.

10 When they were past the first and the second ward, they came unto the iron gate that leadeth unto the city; which opened to them of his own accord: and they went out, and passed on through one street; and forthwith the angel departed from him.

11 And when Peter was come to himself, he said, Now I know of a surety, that the LORD hath sent his angel, and hath delivered me out of the hand of Herod, and from all the expectation of the people of the Jews.
12 And when he had considered the thing, he came to the house of Mary the mother of John, whose surname was Mark; where many were gathered together praying.

13 And as Peter knocked at the door of the gate, a damsel came to hearken, named Rhoda.

14 And when she knew Peter's voice, she opened not the gate for gladness, but ran in, and told how Peter stood before the gate.

15 And they said unto her, Thou art mad. But she constantly affirmed that it was even so. Then said they, It is his angel.

16 But Peter continued knocking: and when they had opened the door, and saw him, they were astonished.

2 Chronicles 7:14
If my people, which are called by my name, shall humble themselves, and pray, and seek my face, and turn from their wicked ways; then will I hear from heaven, and will forgive their sin, and will heal their land.

How Many Times a Day
Should I Pray
Chapter 3

1 Thessalonians 5:17
Pray without ceasing.

Always, throughout the day.
Ephesians 6:18
Praying always with all prayer and supplication in the Spirit, and watching thereunto with all perseverance and supplication for all saints;

Pray all the time. If you're asking for something make sure it's in his will, be consistent, and don't pray selfishly, pray for others while you're praying for yourself.

Jesus said in, Luke 18:1
And he spake a parable unto them to this end, that men ought always to pray, and not to faint;

There is a constant need for prayer. Don't get discouraged or give up, pray until you see it manifest.

Daniel prayed three times a day

Daniel 6:10

Now when Daniel knew that the writing was signed, he went into his house; and his windows being open in his chamber toward Jerusalem, he kneeled upon his knees three times a day, and prayed, and gave thanks before his God, as he did aforetime.

Did Jesus Pray?
Chapter 4

Matthew 11:25-26
[25] *At that time Jesus answered and said, I thank thee, O Father, Lord of heaven and earth, because thou hast hid these things from the wise and prudent, and hast revealed them unto babes.*
[26] *Even so, Father: for so it seemed good in thy sight.*

Matthew 14:23
And when he had sent the multitudes away, he went up into a mountain apart to pray: and when the evening was come, he was there alone.

Mark 1:35
And in the morning, rising up a great while before day, he went out, and departed into a solitary place, and there prayed.

Luke 6:12
And it came to pass in those days, that he went out into a mountain to pray, and continued all night in prayer to God.

People in the Bible Who Prayed
Chapter 5

Abraham
Genesis 18:23-33
And Abraham drew near, and said, Wilt thou also destroy the righteous with the wicked?

24 Peradventure there be fifty righteous within the city: wilt thou also destroy and not spare the place for the fifty righteous that are therein?

25 That be far from thee to do after this manner, to slay the righteous with the wicked: and that the righteous should be as the wicked, that be far from thee: Shall not the Judge of all the earth do right?

26 And the LORD said, If I find in Sodom fifty righteous within the city, then I will spare all the place for their sakes.

27 And Abraham answered and said, Behold now, I have taken upon me to speak unto the LORD, which am but dust and ashes:

²⁸ Peradventure there shall lack five of the fifty righteous: wilt thou destroy all the city for lack of five? And he said, If I find there forty and five, I will not destroy it.

²⁹ And he spake unto him yet again, and said, Peradventure there shall be forty found there. And he said, I will not do it for forty's sake.

³⁰ And he said unto him, Oh let not the L<small>ORD</small> be angry, and I will speak: Peradventure there shall thirty be found there. And he said, I will not do it, if I find thirty there.

³¹ And he said, Behold now, I have taken upon me to speak unto the L<small>ORD</small>: Peradventure there shall be twenty found there. And he said, I will not destroy it for twenty's sake.

³² And he said, Oh let not the L<small>ORD</small> be angry, and I will speak yet but this once: Peradventure ten shall be found there. And he said, I will not destroy it for ten's sake.

³³ And the L<small>ORD</small> went his way, as soon as he had left communing with Abraham: and Abraham returned unto his place.

Hannah

1 Samuel 1:9-18

So Hannah rose up after they had eaten in Shiloh, and after they had drunk. Now Eli the priest sat upon a seat by a post of the temple of the LORD.

10 And she was in bitterness of soul, and prayed unto the LORD, and wept sore.

11 And she vowed a vow, and said, O LORD of hosts, if thou wilt indeed look on the affliction of thine handmaid, and remember me, and not forget thine handmaid, but wilt give unto thine handmaid a man child, then I will give him unto the LORD all the days of his life, and there shall no razor come upon his head.

12 And it came to pass, as she continued praying before the LORD, that Eli marked her mouth.

13 Now Hannah, she spake in her heart; only her lips moved, but her voice was not heard: therefore Eli thought she had been drunken.

14 And Eli said unto her, How long wilt thou be drunken? put away thy wine from thee.

15 And Hannah answered and said, No, my lord, I am a woman of a sorrowful spirit: I have drunk neither wine nor strong drink, but have poured out my soul before the LORD.

¹⁶ Count not thine handmaid for a daughter of Belial: for out of the abundance of my complaint and grief have I spoken hitherto.

¹⁷ Then Eli answered and said, Go in peace: and the God of Israel grant thee thy petition that thou hast asked of him.

¹⁸ And she said, Let thine handmaid find grace in thy sight. So the woman went her way, and did eat, and her countenance was no more sad.

David

2 Samuel 7:18-29
¹⁸ Then went king David in, and sat before the LORD, and he said, Who am I, O Lord GOD? and what is my house, that thou hast brought me hitherto?

¹⁹ And this was yet a small thing in thy sight, O Lord GOD; but thou hast spoken also of thy servant's house for a great while to come. And is this the manner of man, O Lord GOD?

²⁰ And what can David say more unto thee? for thou, Lord GOD, knowest thy servant.

²¹ For thy word's sake, and according to thine own heart, hast thou done all these great things, to make thy servant know them.

*22 Wherefore thou art great, O L*ORD *God: for there is none like thee, neither is there any God beside thee, according to all that we have heard with our ears.*

23 And what one nation in the earth is like thy people, even like Israel, whom God went to redeem for a people to himself, and to make him a name, and to do for you great things and terrible, for thy land, before thy people, which thou redeemedst to thee from Egypt, from the nations and their gods?

*24 For thou hast confirmed to thyself thy people Israel to be a people unto thee forever: and thou, L*ORD, *art become their God.*

*25 And now, O L*ORD *God, the word that thou hast spoken concerning thy servant, and concerning his house, establish it forever, and do as thou hast said.*

*26 And let thy name be magnified forever, saying, The L*ORD *of hosts is the God over Israel: and let the house of thy servant David be established before thee.*

*27 For thou, O L*ORD *of hosts, God of Israel, hast revealed to thy servant, saying, I will build thee an house: therefore hath thy servant found in his heart to pray this prayer unto thee.*

²⁸ And now, O Lord GOD, thou art that God, and thy words be true, and thou hast promised this goodness unto thy servant:

²⁹ Therefore now let it please thee to bless the house of thy servant, that it may continue forever before thee: for thou, O Lord GOD, hast spoken it: and with thy blessing let the house of thy servant be blessed forever.

Solomon

1 Kings 3:5-15
⁵ In Gibeon the LORD appeared to Solomon in a dream by night: and God said, Ask what I shall give thee.

⁶ And Solomon said, Thou hast shewed unto thy servant David my father great mercy, according as he walked before thee in truth, and in righteousness, and in uprightness of heart with thee; and thou hast kept for him this great kindness, that thou hast given him a son to sit on his throne, as it is this day.

⁷ And now, O LORD my God, thou hast made thy servant king instead of David my father: and I am but a little child: I know not how to go out or come in.

⁸ And thy servant is in the midst of thy people which thou hast chosen, a great people, that cannot be numbered nor counted for multitude.

9 Give therefore thy servant an understanding heart to judge thy people, that I may discern between good and bad: for who is able to judge this thy so great a people?

10 And the speech pleased the LORD, that Solomon had asked this thing.

11 And God said unto him, Because thou hast asked this thing, and hast not asked for thyself long life; neither hast asked riches for thyself, nor hast asked the life of thine enemies; but hast asked for thyself understanding to discern judgment;

12 Behold, I have done according to thy words: lo, I have given thee a wise and an understanding heart; so that there was none like thee before thee, neither after thee shall any arise like unto thee.

13 And I have also given thee that which thou hast not asked, both riches, and honour: so that there shall not be any among the kings like unto thee all thy days.

14 And if thou wilt walk in my ways, to keep my statutes and my commandments, as thy father David did walk, then I will lengthen thy days.

15 And Solomon awoke; and, behold, it was a dream. And he came to Jerusalem, and stood before the ark of the covenant of the LORD, and offered up burnt offerings, and offered peace offerings, and made a feast to all his servants.

Jabez

1 Chronicles 4:10
And Jabez called on the God of Israel, saying, Oh that thou wouldest bless me indeed, and enlarge my coast, and that thine hand might be with me, and that thou wouldest keep me from evil, that it may not grieve me! And God granted him that which he requested.

Daniel

Daniel 9:3-15
³ And I set my face unto the Lord God, to seek by prayer and supplications, with fasting, and sackcloth, and ashes:

⁴ And I prayed unto the LORD my God, and made my confession, and said, O Lord, the great and dreadful God, keeping the covenant and mercy to them that love him, and to them that keep his commandments;

⁵ We have sinned, and have committed iniquity, and have done wickedly, and have rebelled, even by departing from thy precepts and from thy judgments:

⁶ Neither have we hearkened unto thy servants the prophets, which spake in thy name to our kings, our princes, and our fathers, and to all the people of the land.

⁷ O LORD, righteousness belongeth unto thee, but unto us confusion of faces, as at this day; to the men of Judah, and to the inhabitants of Jerusalem, and unto all Israel, that are near, and that are far off, through all the countries whither thou hast driven them, because of their trespass that they have trespassed against thee.

⁸ O Lord, to us belongeth confusion of face, to our kings, to our princes, and to our fathers, because we have sinned against thee. ⁹ To the Lord our God belong mercies and forgivenesses, though we have rebelled against him;

¹⁰ Neither have we obeyed the voice of the LORD our God, to walk in his laws, which he set before us by his servants the prophets.

¹¹ Yea, all Israel have transgressed thy law, even by departing, that they might not obey thy voice; therefore the curse is poured upon us, and the oath that is written in the law of Moses the servant of God, because we have sinned against him.

12 And he hath confirmed his words, which he spake against us, and against our judges that judged us, by bringing upon us a great evil: for under the whole heaven hath not been done as hath been done upon Jerusalem.

13 As it is written in the law of Moses, all this evil is come upon us: yet made we not our prayer before the LORD our God, that we might turn from our iniquities, and understand thy truth.

14 Therefore hath the LORD watched upon the evil, and brought it upon us: for the LORD our God is righteous in all his works which he doeth: for we obeyed not his voice.

15 And now, O Lord our God, that hast brought thy people forth out of the land of Egypt with a mighty hand, and hast gotten thee renown, as at this day; we have sinned, we have done wickedly.

Postures in Prayer
Chapter 6

Is there a certain position when talking to the Father?

Bowing

Genesis 24:26
And the man bowed down his head, and worshipped the LORD.

Exodus 4:31
 And the people believed: and when they heard that the LORD had visited the children of Israel, and that he had looked upon their affliction, then they bowed their heads and worshipped.

Kneeling

1 Kings 8:54
And it was so, that when Solomon had made an end of praying all this prayer and supplication unto the LORD, he arose from before the altar of the LORD, from kneeling on his knees with his hands spread up to heaven.

Daniel 6:10
Now when Daniel knew that the writing was

signed, he went into his house; and his windows being open in his chamber toward Jerusalem, he kneeled upon his knees three times a day, and prayed, and gave thanks before his God, as he did aforetime.

Luke 22:41
And he was withdrawn from them about a stone's cast, and kneeled down, and prayed,

Acts 7:60
And he kneeled down, and cried with a loud voice, Lord, lay not this sin to their charge. And when he had said this, he fell asleep.

On Your Face/Prostrate

Numbers 20:6
And Moses and Aaron went from the presence of the assembly unto the door of the tabernacle of the congregation, and they fell upon their faces: and the glory of the LORD appeared unto them.

Joshua 5:14
And he said, Nay; but as captain of the host of the LORD am I now come. And Joshua fell on his face to the earth, and did worship, and said unto him, What saith my Lord unto his servant?

2 Chronicles 20:18
And Jehoshaphat bowed his head with his face to the ground: and all Judah and the

inhabitants of Jerusalem fell before the Lord, worshipping the Lord.

Matthew 26:39
And he went a little farther, and fell on his face, and prayed, saying, O my Father, if it be possible, let this cup pass from me: nevertheless not as I will, but as thou wilt.

Standing

1 Kings 8:22
And Solomon stood before the altar of the Lord in the presence of all the congregation of Israel, and spread forth his hands toward heaven:

Mark 11:25
 And when ye stand praying, forgive, if ye have ought against any: that your Father also which is in heaven may forgive you your trespasses.

Luke 18:11
The Pharisee stood and prayed thus with himself, God, I thank thee, that I am not as other men are, extortioners, unjust, adulterers, or even as this publican.

The Most Powerful Prayer
in the Bible
Chapter 7

Matthew 26:36-44

³⁶ Then cometh Jesus with them unto a place called Gethsemane, and saith unto the disciples, Sit ye here, while I go and pray yonder.
³⁷ And he took with him Peter and the two sons of Zebedee, and began to be sorrowful and very heavy.
³⁸ Then saith he unto them, My soul is exceeding sorrowful, even unto death: tarry ye here, and watch with me.
³⁹ And he went a little farther, and fell on his face, and prayed, saying, O my Father, if it be possible, let this cup pass from me: nevertheless not as I will, but as thou wilt.
⁴⁰ And he cometh unto the disciples, and findeth them asleep, and saith unto Peter, What, could ye not watch with me one hour?
⁴¹ Watch and pray, that ye enter not into temptation: the spirit indeed is willing, but the flesh is weak.
⁴² He went away again the second time, and prayed, saying, O my Father, if this cup may not pass away from me, except I drink it, thy will be done.
⁴³ And he came and found them asleep again: for their eyes were heavy.

44 And he left them, and went away again, and prayed the third time, saying the same words.
John 17:1-26
These words spake Jesus, and lifted up his eyes to heaven, and said, Father, the hour is come; glorify thy Son, that thy Son also may glorify thee:

2 As thou hast given him power over all flesh, that he should give eternal life to as many as thou hast given him.

3 And this is life eternal, that they might know thee the only true God, and Jesus Christ, whom thou hast sent.

4 I have glorified thee on the earth: I have finished the work which thou gavest me to do.

5 And now, O Father, glorify thou me with thine own self with the glory which I had with thee before the world was.

6 I have manifested thy name unto the men which thou gavest me out of the world: thine they were, and thou gavest them me; and they have kept thy word.

7 Now they have known that all things whatsoever thou hast given me are of thee.

8 For I have given unto them the words which thou gavest me; and they have received them, and have known surely that I came out from thee, and they have believed that thou didst send me.

9 I pray for them: I pray not for the world, but for them which thou hast given me; for they are thine.

¹⁰ And all mine are thine, and thine are mine; and I am glorified in them.

¹¹ And now I am no more in the world, but these are in the world, and I come to thee. Holy Father, keep through thine own name those whom thou hast given me, that they may be one, as we are.

¹² While I was with them in the world, I kept them in thy name: those that thou gavest me I have kept, and none of them is lost, but the son of perdition; that the scripture might be fulfilled.

¹³ And now come I to thee; and these things I speak in the world, that they might have my joy fulfilled in themselves.

¹⁴ I have given them thy word; and the world hath hated them, because they are not of the world, even as I am not of the world.

¹⁵ I pray not that thou shouldest take them out of the world, but that thou shouldest keep them from the evil.

¹⁶ They are not of the world, even as I am not of the world.

¹⁷ Sanctify them through thy truth: thy word is truth.

¹⁸ As thou hast sent me into the world, even so have I also sent them into the world.

¹⁹ And for their sakes I sanctify myself, that they also might be sanctified through the truth.

²⁰ Neither pray I for these alone, but for them also which shall believe on me through their word;

²¹ That they all may be one; as thou, Father, art in me, and I in thee, that they also may be one in us: that the world may believe that thou hast sent me.

²² And the glory which thou gavest me I have given them; that they may be one, even as we are one:

²³ I in them, and thou in me, that they may be made perfect in one; and that the world may know that thou hast sent me, and hast loved them, as thou hast loved me.

²⁴ Father, I will that they also, whom thou hast given me, be with me where I am; that they may behold my glory, which thou hast given me: for thou lovedst me before the foundation of the world.

²⁵ O righteous Father, the world hath not known thee: but I have known thee, and these have known that thou hast sent me.

²⁶ And I have declared unto them thy name, and will declare it: that the love wherewith thou hast loved me may be in them, and I in them.

How Long Will It Take for God to Answer
Chapter 8

We must know and remember that the earth is the Lord's and the fullness thereof. Because He created everything and knows everything, He is a God of timing and His timing is perfect.

 We may want what we want right now but God knows what He's doing and He knows the perfect time to bring it forth.

Isaiah 55:8-9
For my thoughts are not your thoughts, neither are your ways my ways, saith the LORD.
⁹ For as the heavens are higher than the earth, so are my ways higher than your ways, and my thoughts than your thoughts.

Ecclesiastes 3:1
"*To everything there is a season, and a time to every purpose under the heaven:*

Habakkuk 2:3
For the vision is yet for an appointed time, but at the end it shall speak, and not lie: though it tarry, wait for it; because it will surely come, it will not tarry.

Proverbs 3:5-6
Trust in the LORD with all thine heart; and lean not unto thine own understanding. 6 In all thy ways acknowledge him, and he shall direct thy paths.

There are so many things that go into our prayers being answered, just to name a few; lessons that God wants us to learn in the midst of our situations, patience, trust, confidence, steadfastness, tolerance, peace, forgiveness, how to wait properly, how to continue to speak life over the situation and how to thank Him in faith until it changes or manifests.

Sometimes our prayers depend upon our maturity to be a good steward and receive the blessing. Sometimes God has to work on the heart of others in order to answer our prayers. Because God is a God of timing and seasons, it must be his divine time and your season for you to be blessed.

I say to you, don't get discouraged when it seems like God has forgotten you, just remember he's at work even when it seems like He's not.

Hebrews 10:36
For ye have need of patience, that, after ye have done the will of God, ye might receive the promise.

When I think about Daniel, he had to wait three weeks before his prayer was manifested.

Daniel 10:2-3;10-14
2 In those days I Daniel was mourning three full weeks.
3 I ate no pleasant bread, neither came flesh nor wine in my mouth, neither did I anoint myself at all, till three whole weeks were fulfilled.
10 And, behold, an hand touched me, which set me upon my knees and upon the palms of my hands.
11 And he said unto me, O Daniel, a man greatly beloved, understand the words that I speak unto thee, and stand upright: for unto thee am I now sent. And when he had spoken this word unto me, I stood trembling.
12 Then said he unto me, Fear not, Daniel: for from the first day that thou didst set thine heart to understand, and to chasten thyself before thy God, thy words were heard, and I am come for thy words.
13 But the prince of the kingdom of Persia withstood me one and twenty days: but, lo, Michael, one of the chief princes, came to help me; and I remained there with the kings of Persia.
14 Now I am come to make thee understand what shall befall thy people in the latter days: for yet the vision is for many days.

Three weeks or three years the best thing we can do is what the psalmist says in Psalms 46:10.

Psalms 46:10
Be still, and know that I am God: I will be exalted among the heathen, I will be exalted in the earth.

How to Pray Properly
Chapter 9

In this last chapter, I will show you how to take the Word of God/ scripture and apply it to your prayer.
If we're going to talk to and with God we must speak His language, and what is his language, His Word.

Morning Prayer
Father,
As I come before your holy presence this morning, I acknowledge you as the giver of life, thanking you for this day. For this is the day, that you have made and I will rejoice and be glad in it. I realize that you have given unto

me all things that pertain unto life and godliness, therefore I thank you, that you have supplied all my need according to your riches in glory by Christ Jesus. I encourage myself this morning by saying, I can do all things through Christ which strengtheneth me. I cover myself as well as my family in the blood of Jesus. Declaring that no weapon formed against us shall prosper. Order my steps this day in Jesus name, for the steps of a good man are ordered by you. In Jesus name Amen!

Scriptures Used:
Psalm 118:24
This is the day which the Lord hath made; we will rejoice and be glad in it.
2 Peter 1:3
According as his divine power hath given unto us all things that pertain unto life and

godliness, through the knowledge of him that hath called us to glory and virtue:

Philippians 4:19
But my God shall supply all your need according to his riches in glory by Christ Jesus.
Philippians 4:13
I can do all things through Christ which strengtheneth me.
Isaiah 54:17
No weapon that is formed against thee shall prosper; and every tongue that shall rise against thee in judgment thou shalt condemn. This is the heritage of the servants of the Lord, and their righteousness is of me, saith the Lord.
Psalm 37:23
The steps of a good man are ordered by the Lord: and he delighteth in his way.

A Prayer of Thanksgiving

Father God, the I AM,
Your Word says in
1 Thessalonians 5:18 In every thing give thanks: for this is the will of God in Christ Jesus concerning me. So I just want to thank you for

life and life more abundantly. (John 10:10)I want to thank you for peace that surpasses all understanding. (Philippians 4:7) I want to thank you that I have no problems because I can cast my cares upon you because you care for me. (1 Peter 5:7) I thank you that no weapon formed against me shall prosper. (Isaiah 54:17)
I thank you that when my ways please you, you'll make my enemies to be at peace with me. (Proverbs 16:7) I thank you that I have favour with you. (Proverbs 12:2)

I thank you for my family, my friends, my job, my home, the fellowship I attend, my pastor, but most of all I thank you for Jesus. IN Jesus name, Amen

A Good Night Prayer

Father, in the name of Jesus as I prepare to lie down for the night, I thank you for all that I have accomplished this day. I thank you for every opportunity to have been a blessing and to have been blessed. Forgive me for every sin I have or may have committed in this day. I thank you that my sleep shall be sweet in Jesus name. Thank you for angels encamped round about me protecting me from all hurt harm and danger. Thank you that you never slumber or sleep, in Jesus name Amen.

Psalm 34:7
The angel of the Lord encampeth round about them that fear him, and delivereth them.

Psalm 121:3
He will not suffer thy foot to be moved: he that
keepeth thee will not slumber.
Proverbs 3:24
When thou liest down, thou shalt not be afraid:
yea, thou shalt lie down, and thy sleep shall be
sweet.

Not Feeling Well

Father, in the name of Jesus, I
thank you that according to 3 John
1:2 you said, "Beloved, I wish
above all things that thou mayest
prosper and be in health, even as
thy soul prospereth." Your Word
says in Isaiah 53:5 "But he was
wounded for our transgressions, he
was bruised for our iniquities: the
chastisement of our peace was
upon him; and with his stripes we
are healed." Because it is your
desire for me to be in health and

Jesus bore the stripes for every manor of sickness and disease, I declare and decree that this sickness must go in the name of Jesus. Give me this wisdom to know what to do according to James 1:5 that says, "If any of you lack wisdom, let him ask of God, that giveth to all men liberally, and upbraideth not; and it shall be given him." In Jesus name Amen.

A Prayer Against the Enemy
Father, in the name of Jesus the Christ, the Mediator, who sits on your right hand interceding for me I come in the power and authority you've given unto me as your daughter/son according to
2 Corinthians 10:3-5 though I walk in the flesh, I do not war after the flesh: For the weapons of our

warfare are not carnal, but mighty through you to the pulling down of strong holds;) Casting down imaginations, and every high thing that exalteth itself against the knowledge of God, and bringing into captivity every thought to the obedience of Christ; I declare and decree according to Isaiah 54:17 No weapon that is formed against me shall prosper; and every tongue that shall rise against me in judgment God shalt condemn. Though I walk in the midst of trouble, thou wilt revive me: thou shalt stretch forth thine hand against the wrath of mine enemies, and thy right hand shall save me, according to Psalms 138:7 I'm glad I know that the angel of the LORD encampeth round about them that fear you, and delivereth them according to Psalms 34:7. Therefore my enemy is defeated in Jesus name, Amen!

A Prayer of Repentance

Father, your Word says, that all have sinned, and come short of your glory; (Romans 3:23) and I have; I seek your forgiveness according to 1John 1:9 that says, If I confess my sins, you are faithful and just to forgive my sins, and to cleanse me from all unrighteousness. In Acts 3:19 your word says, "Repent ye therefore, and be converted, that your sins may be blotted out, when the times of refreshing shall come from the presence of the Lord." Deliver me O God that I might be able to say like the Apostle Paul, "When I was a child, I spake as a child, I understood as a child, I thought as a child: but when I became a man, I put away childish things. (1 Corinthians 13:11)" For I want to be pleasing in your sight. For "When a man's ways please the Lord, he maketh even his enemies to be at peace with him" according to Proverbs 16:7 in Jesus name Amen!

Now that you know everything you need to know about how to properly talk to God, let's get started and change some things, situations and lives by what we say to God. Amen? Amen!

About the Author

Dr. Ruth Wilson is the pastor and founder of the Shekinah Glory International Ministries located in Louisville, KY. She is not one who likes to talk about herself but she says, "let the work I do, speak for me."

Dr. Ruth operates in each of the fivefold ministry (pastor, teacher, evangelist, prophet and apostle) as God desires to use her according of the needs of each assignment.

She knows firsthand how low the enemy will go in an attempt to destroy and abort God's divine purpose for one's life.

Dr. Ruth is a true intercessor and prayer warrior, living proof that some things only come through fasting and prayer.

Her travels has taken her throughout the United States to Auckland, New Zealand to Port au Prince, Haiti where hundreds were delivered and gave their lives to the Lord.

Dr. Ruth is on a personal mission to expose the enemy for who and what he is; a LIAR and a THIEF.

She believes that once we know the truth we can't help but be free and walk in the fullness of who God says we are, doing what He says what we can do and receive what He says we can have.

64

"And ye shall know the truth, and the truth shall make you free."
John 8:32 (KJV)

God is not a respecter of persons. What He does for one, He will do for another; He'll do it for you.

Let us know, tell someone else, or if you would like to order additional copies send all correspondence to:

Dr. Ruth is also available as a speaker at your next revival, conference or workshop. Contact her at:

Dr. Ruth Wilson
P. O. Box 133
Louisville, KY 40201
Email us at:
dauparoom@yahoo.com